Okapi

Sara Antill

WINDMILL
BOOKS

New York

Published in 2011 by Windmill Books, LLC
303 Park Avenue South, Suite # 1280, New York, NY 10010-3657

First Edition

CREDITS:
Author: Sara Antill
Edited by: Jennifer Way
Designed by: Brian Garvey

Photo Credits: Cover (okapi, background), backcover, pp. 5 (right, left), 7, 9, 12, 14, 16 (inset), 16-17, 20, 22 (bottom) Shutterstock.com; pp. 4-5 Martin Harvey/Getty Images; p. 6 (main) © www.iStockphoto.com/Yves Grau; p. 6 (inset) © www.iStockphoto.com/Natural_Warp; p. 8 © www.iStockphoto.com/Humberto Vidal; p. 10 (left) © www.iStockphoto.com/Gary Martin; p. 10 (right) © www.iStockphoto.com/Melissa Englert; p. 11 © www.iStockphoto.com/Graffizone; p. 13 (main) Stan Osolinski/Getty Images; pp. 13 (inset), 22 (top) © www.iStockphoto.com/Nancy Nehring; pp. 14-15 © www.iStockphoto.com/Guenter Guni; p. 18 © SuperStock, Inc.; p. 19 Jim Watson/AFP/Getty Images; p. 21 John Moore/Getty Images.

Library of Congress Cataloging-in-Publication Data

Antill, Sara.
 Okapi / by Sara Antill. — 1st ed.
     p. cm. — (Unusual animals)
 Includes index.
 ISBN 978-1-60754-996-3 (library binding) — ISBN 978-1-61533-007-2 (pbk.) — ISBN 978-1-61533-008-9 (6-pack)
 1. Okapi. I. Title.
 QL737.U56A68 2011
 599.638—dc22

                          2010006167

Manufactured in the United States of America

For more great fiction and nonfiction, go to windmillbooks.com.

CPSIA Compliance Information: Batch # BW2011WM: For Further Information contact Windmill Books, New York, New York at 1-866-478-0556

Table of Contents

African Mystery

The okapi is an unusual animal, but it may look familiar. That's because its body looks a lot like the body of a horse, and it has stripes that make it look like a zebra. But the okapi's closest **relative** is actually the giraffe.

One hundred years ago, most people in the world didn't know that the okapi existed. For many years, it was called the "African unicorn" because it was such a mystery!

The okapi has stripes like a zebra, but it is more closely related to the giraffe.

Giraffe

Zebra

Okapis live in the rain forests of central Africa. Rain forests are warm areas with lots of trees and plenty of rain.

The Nyungwe forest is in Rwanda. This is part of the area in central Africa where okapis live.

A full-grown okapi can measure about 8 feet (2.5 m) long and 5 feet (1.5 m) tall. It can weigh around 440 to 660 pounds (200–300 kg). This is about the same size as a small horse.

When we see an okapi's black-and-white stripes, we may think that they make the animal stand out. In the rain forest, though, these stripes help the okapi to hide using **camouflage**!

The okapi's stripes help it to blend in with its surroundings.

Animals that live in rain forests, like the okapi, use camouflage to help them hide from animals that want to eat them.

In the rain forest, tall trees block much of the sunlight from getting through. Because of this, the forest floor can be very dark. When rays of light do shine though the trees, they look just like the okapi's stripes.

Some Tongue!

Male okapis have two bony bumps on their heads, just as giraffes do.

Ossicones

The short horn-like bumps are called **ossicones**. They are covered with skin and fur.

Another thing okapis have in common with giraffes is their long, blue tongue.

An okapi's tongue can be as long as 18 inches (46 cm). It is one of the longest tongues of any **mammal** in the world. In fact, it's so long, an okapi can clean its ears with it!

This okapi is feeding on grass. Okapis are plant-eaters, and do not eat meat.

Okapis are most active in the afternoon and early evening. They can travel more than half a mile (0.8 km) every day, looking for food.

Okapis eat mostly leaves, twigs, grass, and fruit. They use their long tongues to tear leaves off trees. Okapis also eat **charcoal** and clay. They can eat 40 to 65 pounds (18–29 kg) of food every day!

The okapi's long tongue helps it to reach for food.

Most okapis like to live alone. They like to have their own space, but they will usually let other okapis pass though their territory without any trouble. Small groups will even eat together sometimes.

These two okapis are feeding together peacefully.

The Okapi Wildlife Reserve is in the Democratic Republic of Congo. The reserve is in a rain forest near Rwenzori mountain, shown here.

Okapis have a scent **gland** on each of their feet. This gland leaves a sticky trail on the ground wherever the okapi steps. This lets other okapis know that another okapi was there first!

Okapis have large ears that stand upward. This gives them a very good sense of hearing. They can usually hear a predator, like a leopard, coming from far away.

Leopard

Their excellent sense of hearing lets these okapis know if they are in danger.

When an okapi is in danger, it will
try to hide behind trees and plants.
If it cannot hide, it may try to run away.

Baby Okapi

Baby okapis weight about 50 pounds (23 kg). A young okapi will be able to stand up just 30 minutes after it is born. It will be fully grown by the time it is 3 years old.

This young okapi is resting in the grass. It still has a fringe of black hair on its back.

Young okapis look a lot like their parents. They are born with a **fringe** of hair that runs along their back. This disappears by the time they are one year old.

A mother okapi looks after her baby until it is about three years old.

A mother okapi will hide her babies in a nest. They will stay there for the first two months of their life.

It is against the law to hunt okapis, but some people break these laws.

There are laws in Africa that are meant to protect the okapi. However, some people don't follow these laws. Okapis are in danger from hunting and loss of **habitat**.

In 1952, part of the Ituri Forest, where the okapis live, was set aside as a **wildlife reserve**. The Okapi Wildlife Reserve is a place where okapis, as well as the other plants and animals that live and grow there, can be safe from danger.

Part of this rain forest was burned down to make room for farms. This is one way in which okapis have lost some of their habitat.

Inside Story

In a zoo, an okapi can live up to 30 years.

Male okapis are usually smaller than females.

The okapi was first called an "atti." People thought it might be a kind of donkey!

Glossary

CAMOUFLAGE (KAM-uh-flaj) To hide by blending in with the surroundings.

CHARCOAL (CHAR-kowl) Burned wood that has turned into solid carbon.

FRINGE (FRINJ) A strip or thin line of something, like hair.

GLAND (GLAND) An organ that releases fluid or smell.

HABITAT (HA-bih-tat) The kind of environment where an animal or plant naturally lives.

MAMMAL (MA-mul) A warm-blooded animal that has a backbone and hair, breathes air, and feeds milk to its young.

OSSICONE (AH-sih-kown) A bony bump, covered with skin.

RELATIVE (REH-luh-tiv) An animal that closely resembles another animal genetically.

WILDLIFE RESERVE (WYLD-lyf ree-zerv) An area of nature set aside for plants and animals to grow where they are safe from humans.

Index

Read More

Pohl, Kathleen. *Looking at the Congo*. Strongsville, OH: Gareth Stevens Publishing, 2008.

Ryan-Herndon, Lisa. *Animals of Africa*. New York: Scholastic, Inc., 2008.

Steele, Christy. *Okapis*. Chicago: Raintree, 2003.

Web Sites

For Web resources related to the subject of this book, go to: www.windmillbooks.com/weblinks and select this book's title.